PRAISE FOR *HOW TO WORK FROM HOME AND ACTUALLY GET SH*T DONE*

"Sound practical advice which should help employees and managers adjust to our new normal."

—*Jeff Yasuda, CEO and cofounder, Feed.fm*

"Cynthia's sense of humor and down-to-earth approach shows that, when it comes to virtual team success, being aware of remote team distractions and accommodating this pays off."

—*Cody Lohnes, Partner, Grant Thornton LLP*

"Cynthia's focused fifty tips are stellar guides for your virtual teams' success!"

—*Marcia Daszko, leadership and business strategist, virtual and global speaker, and bestselling author*

"A pragmatic approach to the complexities of working virtually. I have no doubt this should help employees and managers adjust to the new way of distributed work and projects."

—*Suzanne Marineau, thirty-five-year human resources executive*

"Trying to understand the nuances of remote work is probably the most common pain point businesses are feeling in 2020. Luckily, Cynthia has broken it down into pieces we can understand. Thank you!"

—*Tom Kostandoff "TK", forty-seven-year capital markets executive and past president, ZSA-X Financial Services Recruitment*

"Having worked with Cynthia and knowing how much of her passion went into this book, I can honestly say I am so excited to see this come to fruition. Mixing business with unabashed wit and charm, her book may be the most fun way to save remote teams from themselves."

—*Chala Dincoy-Flajnik, author, marketing coach, and CEO and founder of The Repositioning Expert*

"Having experienced the revenue and productivity gains of Virtira's sales support division (Sales Beacon) with a past employer, I can attest that the methods Cynthia describes to increase remote work performance are very effective!"

—*Kelly Carlberg, Global Sales, Video Surveillance & IOT, Dell Technologies*

HOW TO WORK FROM HOME AND ACTUALLY GET SH*T DONE

50 TIPS FOR LEADERS AND PROFESSIONALS
TO WORK REMOTELY AND OUTPERFORM THE OFFICE

HOW TO WORK FROM HOME AND ACTUALLY GET SH*T DONE

CYNTHIA D. SPRAGGS

CEO, VIRTIRA.COM

Advantage®

Published by Advantage, Charleston, South Carolina.
Member of Advantage Media Group.

ADVANTAGE is a registered trademark, and the Advantage colophon is a trademark of Advantage Media Group, Inc.

Printed in the United States of America.

10 9 8 7 6 5 4 3 2 1

ISBN: 978-1-64225-223-1
LCCN: 2020913164

Book design by Carly Blake.

This publication is designed to provide accurate and authoritative information in regard to the subject matter covered. It is sold with the understanding that the publisher is not engaged in rendering legal, accounting, or other professional services. If legal advice or other expert assistance is required, the services of a competent professional person should be sought.

Advantage Media Group is proud to be a part of the Tree Neutral® program. Tree Neutral offsets the number of trees consumed in the production and printing of this book by taking proactive steps such as planting trees in direct proportion to the number of trees used to print books. To learn more about Tree Neutral, please visit **www.treeneutral.com**.

Advantage Media Group is a publisher of business, self-improvement, and professional development books and online learning. We help entrepreneurs, business leaders, and professionals share their Stories, Passion, and Knowledge to help others Learn & Grow. Do you have a manuscript or book idea that you would like us to consider for publishing? Please visit **advantagefamily.com** or call **1.866.775.1696**.

To Graham, my soul mate and global adventure partner. Not once, across so many destinations, has there been one sign of discontent with my laptop emerging from my backpack at some teensy time in the morning to jump on a call or do a few hours of work. Thank you.

CONTENTS

THE SHORTEST COMMUTE IN THE WORLD

B efore the coronavirus pandemic, most of us were already accustomed to doing some light work from home. Answering emails, calls, maybe even polishing a report or doing some online research ... simple after-hours tasks that could be quickly accomplished.

But none of us were prepared for what came our way in early 2020.

The COVID-19 crisis forced many of us to work full-time without ever leaving home. And not only were employees not prepared for this major life switch—neither were our employers! Many companies became obsessed with maintaining their brick-and-mortar culture despite the fact their offices were completely deserted. I heard several horror stories about companies mandating that employees eat lunch on camera or play bar games with cocktails on Zoom after an exhausting workday.

Not only were these extra obligations not necessary, but they got in the way of harried workers just trying to structure and maintain their new lives. After all, many of them also had to take care of their now-homeschooled kids, deal with pets excited to have their masters around 24/7, and juggle schedules with spouses who were also now working full-time from home. They also had to deal with various other temptations that come along with being house-bound—such as that big-screen TV and comfy couch beckoning their owners to crash and binge the latest Netflix sensation instead of deal with last month's financials.

As I write these words, some companies are reopening their doors. There is the possibility that hybrid workforces will be the new normal, simply because it's more productive for all parties, not to mention greener for the planet. Whatever the case, if you're someone who's new to doing their entire job remotely—or if you're one of many bosses who find themselves suddenly overseeing an army of home workers—this is the book for you.

As you might have read on the front cover, my name is Cynthia Spraggs, and I'm an expert on virtual work. And believe me, I practice what I preach—after all, I've been working remotely since I was ten years old. In the '60s, I did data entry from my brother's home office in Palo Alto, which was hooked up via telephone acoustic coupler to the legendary DCD 6600 at Stanford. Later, in the '80s, I worked as a sales engineer from my own home office, where my little portable Texas Instrument Silent 700 terminal could link up to IBM's massive 360 supercomputer.

After I wrote my master's thesis on telecommuting in 1993, I vowed never to work in an office because, frankly, I found offices very inefficient. After the kerfuffle of getting ready, then the long commute, you had coffee breaks, lunch breaks, people dropping by and chatting—it was difficult to accomplish very much. So, since 1993, I've worked from home and from all over the world, including Machu Pichu, Patagonia, the Galapagos, and even at the base camp of Mount Everest. Currently, as president and CEO of Virtira, a company that makes virtual business more effective—in fact, we guarantee it—I lead a team of consultants who implement process, standardized tools, and facilitation to make sure that everyone, whether they're across the street or across the world, stays on track and accountable. We've found that the best way to guarantee successful virtual meetings, projects, and events is to make sure people work as efficiently as possible and achieve the best result from each workday. In other words, we help them "get sh*t done." As a result, we've helped Fortune 500 companies be more productive, drive more revenue, and obtain better ROI in over one thousand assignments.

> **We've found that the best way to guarantee successful virtual meetings, projects, and events is to make sure people work as efficiently as possible and achieve the best result from each workday.**

If you've made the shift to working (or managing) from home, you may often feel isolated, as if no one is paying attention to what you're doing or what you're trying to communicate. You might expect me to say at this point, "Oh, don't be silly." Well, you're not being silly. On the contrary, you *need* to assume no one hears you and conduct business accordingly. Which means you have to recalibrate, regroup, and do things a little differently—because the good news is there are *specific actions* you can take to stay engaged, stay focused, and get the job done, even though you may now be doing that job on the kitchen counter of your apartment!

I'm going to assume you already have access to the tech stack[1] you need to get the job done and know how to manage your own work (and possibly the work of others). With that in place, the idea of this book is to help you maximize your productivity without the benefit of being physically inside an office environment. To that end, I've dug into our consulting practice and "mined" fifty short actionable tips for working, communications, online meetings, and cross-functional team management to make you productive with as little stress as possible. This way, you'll survive future disruptions in style.

I truly hope your remote working experience is a positive one and leads to much success for you in the future.

Best,

Cynthia

---

1   The tech stack is the set of tools that makes remote work possible: Videoconferencing, chat, internal dashboards, ideation, and spreadsheet/word processing solutions (Zoom/Slack/Smartsheet/Miro/Office 365). Unfortunately, an unannounced update of one of these tools can make it go sideways, usually in the middle of an important meeting.

CHAPTER 1

HOME ALONE: GETTING DOWN TO BUSINESS

R eady to wade through one hundred thousand emails a day while your children smear chocolate on your keyboard and try a variety of funny hats on your head? Or hop on an important video conference while your dog brings up breakfast on the floor behind you?

Of course you are!

Or you will be, after you attend to a few simple tips that will make your entire online working life easier. A *lot* easier. Here we go ...

TIP #1: INVEST IN A GREAT HEADSET

If you can't be heard during online meetings, you aren't going to be very impressive to management or your coworkers. This is *not* the time to use those off-brand headsets you picked up at the Dollar Store or your PC microphone. Let everyone else's voice drop in and out or crackle with static; you want to sound clear as a bell. That's why your first priority when working from home should be to invest in a good headset and, just as importantly, a backup in case there's a problem. And please, don't rely on Bluetooth buds—because, unfortunately, batteries go bad just when you need them the most. If you're a manager, dip into that unused travel budget and upgrade everyone's gear (for ideas, check out our "2020 Headset Rankings" at virtira.com/resources).

TIP #2: CONSIDER THE WEBCAM OPTIONAL

During the pandemic, you've no doubt witnessed many a multiheaded screen, either through participating in Zoom calls or watching commercials that make fun of them. You've probably also contracted a different illness I call "Zoom Fatigue," which causes headaches from squinting at those tiny boxes and trying to figure out who's who ... especially if the guys have quit shaving.

Why are so many remote workers forced to do video meetings? Because someone (most likely a person who never worked remotely before) has confused the concept of *building relationships with actually getting something done*.

On one level, I get it. Most who worked in offices are used to physically seeing other people, so, since the technology is available, why not do video interaction so there's still some face time involved? The truth is that aspect of webcams *is* important for team bonding, but here's a way to balance the social with the practical: everyone keep their webcams on for maybe three minutes or so to start a videoconference, then step back and let the person running the meeting (or someone presenting content) take up the whole screen.

Many people feel group pressure to keep their webcams on. As an exercise, why not do an anonymous poll and just see how many see the benefit of a bunch of talking heads? Make being on camera a fun team-building exercise rather than an obligation (wear a funny hat to work day, bring your pet to the office day).

Frankly, unless it's a team-building exercise,

there is *no* reason for everyone's head to be visible the whole time. All that does is make people feel obligated to stare at their webcams during the entire meeting, so they look like they're listening. Now, imagine a large in-person meeting where everybody stared at everyone else in the same way. That would be just plain creepy! In a conference room setting, people are generally looking down at their notepads or printed material. They don't stare each other down like Keanu Reeves and whoever he's going to shoot next in a John Wick movie.

TIP #3: MASTER YOUR ONLINE MEETING TOOLS

Whichever video conferencing system you and your coworkers use, just make sure you have better than average skills on all the bells and whistles. Better yet, become proficient on a number of different online meeting platforms. You don't want to spend fifteen minutes at the start of a meeting trying to figure out how to unmute someone you've accidentally muted like I did on a new platform we were testing last week. And you *definitely* don't want to be the person shouting "Hello? Hello? *Hello?*" into your mic.

Practice makes perfect. Encourage everyone to lead a call and present at least twice a month, so each one of you knows how to record meetings, use rotating intro slides, do online polls and voting, manage breakout sessions, and hide the meeting participants list. This last one is especially useful if you're doing a three-hundred-person invite launch and only five people show up.

You should also know how to recover from screen freezes and bandwidth crashes for yourself and others on your team (hint: make sure more than one person has a copy of your presentation so they can click through slides while you talk on audio only).

If you use PowerPoint, everyone should know how to use presenter mode because you don't want to share the wrong window with all your secret notes showing (hint: it always defaults to the wrong one!). And never share your screen if there's a possibility that your dating site could notify you of new matches during your meeting with the CEO.

TIP #4: MAKE SURE YOUR TECH IS TIGHT

Just how old is your PC or Apple? How well is it running? Is there plenty of RAM and space on the hard drive? How long has it been since you updated critical programs? This last question is particularly important, since the last thing you need thirty seconds before an important call or video presentation is a frozen screen courtesy of a massive Windows update that will require a complete reboot of your computer.

Hopefully, there's a department or third party who's handling this incredibly important piece of your remote worker puzzle. Whether they do it or you do it, make sure your browsers are routinely wiped of auto-fill passwords, cookies, and trackers and your antivirus software is beefed up and updated.

Nothing ruins your day like being the source of the Trojan horse that corrupts the entire corporate security infrastructure.

And lose the nonwork social media sites and computer games. Nothing ruins your day like being the source of the Trojan horse that corrupts the entire corporate security infrastructure.

TIP #5: KEEP IT ALL IN THE CLOUD

Ready to welcome a nightmare into your home office? Here's an easy way to do it: store all your work information on your PC's hard drive. Local storage of company data is not only a security risk; it can cause many an operational migraine. Don't waste a ton of time diligently working on an old file you saved on your computer when there's an updated version available online. You'll find yourself weeping quietly into your hands because you now have to do that work all over again.

The *only time* you should have a document on your computer is if you are presenting on a meeting. If there's a glitch with cloud access, at least everyone won't be staring at a blank screen while you try to retrieve the file.

Also, make sure that someone does regular physical backups of your cloud data. We've had our information corrupted and rendered completely irretrievable by one of the big online services—if not for that daily physical backup, we would have lost years of data. That's why we double back up *everything*!

TIP #6: STAKE YOUR CLAIM TO BANDWIDTH

Make sure your bandwidth is as fast and furious as possible. You want to be able to present, share, and interact with people without your audio fading in and out. This may mean turning off your virtual private network (VPN)[2] before an important presentation.

---

2   A virtual private network is a software program that adds extra security when online by masking your location. Sometimes these same systems can drop your wireless speeds to a slow crawl.

The problem might not be with your internet as much as it is with those other people who live with you, if they're clogging up the connection with their smartphones or endless Netflix binges. Solve that ongoing problem by creating separate bandwidth-limited Wi-Fi channels, so you can have that big bad broadband all to yourself (but maybe share a little with your spouse to keep things congenial!).

TIP #7: DON'T TAKE SECURITY RISKS

In many a spy film, there's a character that orders their men to "secure the perimeter." That's to prevent the hero from infiltrating the villain's base, which that hero is going to do anyway, because otherwise, there's no movie. Well, you also have to secure your "perimeter"—i.e., your home computer setup—so nobody invades your cyberspace. Because, odds are, it won't be a hero making the attempt.

Remote work increases security risks. The difference between the protection offered by big data pipes with secured lines into office buildings versus the protection offered by a home PC connection is drastic. The potential for hacking, viruses, and ransomware increases tenfold when you're a remote worker.

Aside from having your VPN in place, get a

password management system like LastPass, Keeper, or Dashlane, and implement it immediately. Don't use browser-based password storage or auto-complete systems. These are a hacker's dream and your company's nightmare, because home networks are so much easier to break into than office networks.

*Cynthia catching up on emails at
Everest Base Camp, 2007.*

CHAPTER 2

GO PRO: WORKING IN YOUR PJS

Working at home is a challenge simply because … well, you're at home. And at home, you're used to doing whatever you want behind your own front door. That's why introducing a forty-hour workweek into your personal arena can really throw you off your game. Here are some simple suggestions on how to make you an online professional rock star, even though your cat and kids may be less than supportive of the "new you."

TIP #8: DODGE DISORDER WITH DASHBOARDS

Dashboards are essential for keeping everyone informed and on track—you can check your action items, everyone else's action items, status reporting, who is slacking and who's killing it, as well as risks, blockages, and links to any departmental information and templates you need to find.

Most importantly, you can do this instantly, 24/7.

Figure 1 shows examples of dashboards that we use to keep client departments and projects on track. Some companies use Confluence or Basecamp; we use Smartsheets. You can create them using a free account and wow everyone with your new online organizational skills. Truly, dashboards will transform your life.

Examples of Dashboards

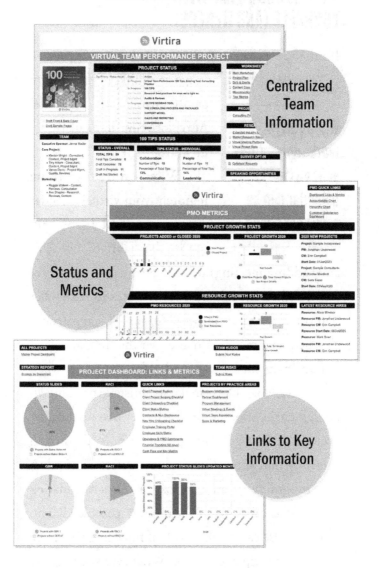

Figure 1. Dashboard examples
from Virtira.com/resources

TIP #9: BOOK TIME WITH YOURSELF (AND OTHERS)

If other people have the ability to book meetings on your calendar, block off regular chunks of time so you can control your schedule. Also block time to regularly get up and stretch.

When you're working remotely, your virtual calendar can be your best friend.

When you're working remotely, your virtual calendar can be your best friend. So, get in the habit of immediately adding meetings to your calendar when they're scheduled. Don't rely on Post-it Notes to remember that you've got a meeting at 10:00 a.m. When you need to schedule a meeting, nail down the time and send out an invite after everyone has let you know when they're available. Don't make the mistake of doing an endless chain of back-and-forth over potential times, because people will end up confused. And you will probably find yourself in that same state of mind. A better solution? Invest in a cross-platform calendaring tool so you can stay out of the fray completely and someone else can do the work of finalizing the time.

A bonus tip about time: Whenever you're going to be away a half day or longer, set your email to send out an auto-reply "Out of Office" message so that people off your network can plan around your response time. For multiday absences, set an auto reply and a vacation banner in whatever tool you're using so people don't expect to hear from you.

TIP #10: SHOW EVERYONE THE DOOR

If your home office space is limited, I sympathize. But I also *strongly* advise you to find a way to put a door between you and the rest of the household if you don't live alone. While it's webcam cute if your kitty lies down on your desk and purrs for all to enjoy, it's not so cute if your feline friend starts coughing up a fur ball while you're making a virtual presentation. Shut the door and stick a sign on the outside of it: "SHHH. IMPORTANT PERSON AT WORK." Hopefully, your spouse won't laugh loudly at it while you're on the phone ...

TIP #11: AN OFFICE IS AN OFFICE IS AN OFFICE

Do yourself a favor. Print out the title of this tip (inspired by Gertrude Stein) and stick it on the wall above your monitor in order to remind yourself that, even though you're at home, you're also at work. Yes, your office is now at home, but you still have to *act* like it's an office. You'll still be interacting with colleagues, and you'll still be expected to respond to messages in a timely manner—not to mention actually getting your work done. Joining a management meeting on camera in your fluffy PJs while eating your breakfast cereal and wearing a bunny hat to celebrate your home-based freedom is not adorable. Stay professional—and stay employed.

TIP #12: WORK YOUR "LOOK"

You are your own brand—and you want to rock that brand. So, if you're doing regular video conferences, do a little work on what other people are going to see of you and your surroundings.

Consider using a separate webcam on a tripod and put tape over the one on your monitor if you don't want it accidentally turning on. Think about your lighting—are you in shadows from a window behind you? Make sure your entire head is in the frame and not just the top of your head, so you don't look like an extra from *The Blair Witch Project*. Have a team-building exercise to discover exactly what level the camera should be at. Convention says eye level, but many on my team argue that chin level is more flattering.

When we're not meeting people in person, we have to work a little harder to make connections, so don't be afraid to showcase positive aspects of your personality. These personal touches can stimulate conversation outside the bounds of work and create stronger virtual connections. Express who you are. If you play guitar, or if you're like me and you have five guitars and hope they will magically learn to play themselves, go ahead and hang them on the wall. Children's art, your art, a surfboard, a photo of a place you really love … think about what conveys who you are and your interests—so you can visually express this as part of your online persona. If your background is a mess, get one of those old slide projection screens, then let your kids paint it and put it behind you.

TIP #13: DRESS FOR THE UNEXPECTED

Near the start of the pandemic, a reporter for *Good Morning America* popped up from his home to introduce a story. He looked good, this reporter did, wearing a splendid coat and tie. Unfortunately, the way his webcam was angled, you could also plainly see he was wearing shorts!

For virtual workers, especially if you deal directly with customers or are on lots of on-camera calls with executives, you want to look and sound like a pro. Always strive to create the best possible first impression. And *always* be camera ready from head to foot. Think about how embarrassed you might be if some kind of household emergency causes you to rush off in the middle of your video conference and everyone sees you run away in your Joe Boxers—you know, the ones with the hearts …

CHAPTER 3

COMMUNICATING DOS AND DON'TS

et's talk about cats.

Specifically, let's talk about ten cats who spend the day in a ten by ten room (and please, let's not focus on the resulting smell of that situation). Somehow, you've managed to be a top cat wrangler—you've trained these fantastic felines to work together and do various jobs. They all get along great, and they get those jobs done, because they operate as a team.

Now … take those same cats and put them out in a random field somehow. All of a sudden, it doesn't matter how well they worked together in that small room or how tight a team they were then, because now those cats are going to be running around completely distracted by everything going on outside. They'll be chasing butterflies, chasing mice, and getting lost in the weeds. What they won't be doing is worrying about what those other cats are up to.

Well, it's the same with a virtual team. While you may have worked terrifically in an office environment, at home, between all your social media feeds, cooking shows, dating sites, DNA results, kids, pets, and everything else going on, you (as well as everyone else) are going to end up being distracted. *A lot.* That's why you cool cats have to work overtime to keep connected and stay on the same page—and that means sharpening your communication skills accordingly.

Here are a few ways to get that done.

TIP #14: APPLY WIIFM TO ALL COMMUNICATIONS

Short-circuit short attention spans! Have you ever gotten a lengthy message or voice mail that takes *way* too much time to wade through, and by the end of it you realize it has very little relevance to you?

No one has time to deal with this. Learn the concept of WIIFM (what's in it for me) and focus your messages on what your readers or listeners care about. They will engage more with your communication if it makes their lives easier.

This also means sticking to the point, because one of the things they care about is understanding your communication as quickly as possible. When you're communicating with people online, particularly if they're busy, don't add a lot of gobbledygook. Be direct and organized, avoid adjectives and adverbs, and tailor it to their needs.

Nobody needs overwritten, flowery language. Everyone just wants to get down to brass tacks so they can move on with their work. Consider gifting everyone on your team the best guide on succinct communications ever written, *The Elements of Style*, by William Strunk Jr.

TIP #15: USE THE BILLBOARD CONCEPT FOR DATA

As noted in the last tip, you want to get to the point quickly—and that extends to how you disseminate data and information. Whether it's financials, metrics, data analysis, or reporting, you want to make it easy for people to understand the bottom line quickly, especially since you're communicating virtually.

That's why I suggest the billboard analogy— imagine you have the time it takes for someone to drive past a billboard to make your point. With that in mind, think about what you need to convey, put that front and center, and make it visually engaging. If you can catch their attention, they'll note it and dig into the data if it is of interest.

How to Show Data More Effectively

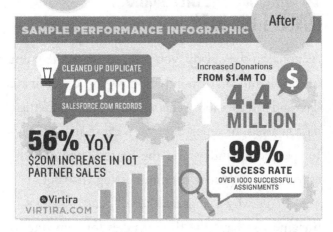

Figure 2. Reporting before-and-after example

Figure 2 illustrates what I'm talking about. Put your focus on selling ideas and telling compelling stories by summarizing the key takeaways. Don't overdo it on the data unless you're trying to bury something nasty under all the numbers.

Data visualization becomes much more important when you're working remotely. Be simple, succinct, and visual when possible. And also expect the information to be forwarded—so make it something your grandmother would understand.

TIP #16: KEEP SMALL TALK SMALL

There's a difference between personal and professional conversations, and both are important in their own way. Personal ones are obviously more helpful in building relationships, whether they're with employees, coworkers, or customers. That kind of casual talk works best as people are joining a call—but you want to try to limit it to around three minutes, depending on the size of the group (if you must use webcams, this would be the time to do it, as I mentioned earlier).

But when you go longer than that three minutes, it starts to create issues.

First of all, when there's too much small talk at the start of a meeting, people will begin jumping on later and later, because they know nobody will get down to business very quickly. It's like getting to a movie late because you know they're going to show thirty trailers and commercials beforehand.

And one more thing about how you talk the talk. You (and everyone else) need to know that many of these calls are recorded—and what is said on them will hold up in court (a Perry Mason moment avoided). So be careful. If you're not sure about the language you're about to use, go out of your way to keep it on the safe side. Even if you're joking, someone else might not think so—after all, body language is hard to read when you can't see the person's body!

> **Body language is hard to read when you can't see the person's body!**

TIP #17: WATCH OUT FOR WHOOPSIES

When sending out business messages, it's not enough to be just *careful*. You have to be **CAREFUL**. Because you never know what could happen.

A friend of mine, in the early days of faxing from personal computers, used a border of "WingDings" on their fax cover sheet. He thought he was being funny when he spelled out various obscenities with the WingDings font—after all, even though you use letters on the keyboard to type them, they appear on screen and paper as abstract symbols. Ha, ha, right? Well, what my friend didn't know was that all fonts were converted to a single default font when the computer sent the fax ... meaning his client saw a whole line of swear words at the top of the fax.

That's a big whoopsie.

But it just goes to show you that when you fool around, the joke could be on you. Context, normally gleaned by facial expressions, vocal tone, and body language, can be much more ambiguous online. A remark that, when delivered face-to-face, might be construed as friendly feedback or a humorous comment might sound harsh and serious when sent in a message. Any of these could start a downward spiral into a Twitterverse-like hell that would be incredibly difficult to emerge from.

So, make a point of putting a positive spin on whatever you're writing. Lower the attitude if you're pointing out problems and be more encouraging than discouraging. And on your side, try not to take anything personally. If you sense hostility, find a nice or humorous way to address it. And again, don't be afraid to pick up the phone and talk it out with someone if you feel the air needs to be cleared.

TIP #18: USE EMAIL SPARINGLY

There's nothing like communicating with everyone online to understand the baffling ball of confusion that email can easily create.

Just like the famous *I Love Lucy* episode where Lucy and Ethel desperately try to keep up with an assembly line of chocolates that keep coming down the belt with increasing speed, emails can pour into your inbox to the point where you can't keep them straight. Your work emails can also easily get lost in a sea of spam and a myriad of other messages. Even if you have a dedicated work email server, you'll find important information easily gets lost in the middle of endless threads on the same email.

There's also the dicey situation of sending an email, realizing you wrote exactly the *wrong* thing, and being unable to retract and rewrite the message. Once you hit the "send" button, you're usually helpless to get it back. And that can add up to a huge problem for you if there are words you should have kept to yourself. Worse yet, that problematic email can be forwarded to others, including your boss, or posted on social media. There are better ways of building your fifteen seconds of fame.

So, be smart about how you use email. Instead,

encourage everyone to rely on messaging systems like MS Teams, Webex Teams, or Slack, because they let you easily follow conversations, engage groups of people, and find the nuggets of info you need much more efficiently.

These kinds of collaboration platforms also let you retract messages, which can save you a lot of grief. I've seen how using messaging instead of email can cut down team conflict significantly—simply because any heat-of-the-moment "zingers" can go away with a click.

TIP #19: OKAY, BUT IF YOU DO USE EMAIL ...

Although email is a killer to productivity, there are still ways to maximize its effectiveness, so the last part of this chapter covers this. You may need email to document things in writing with a time stamp. Or, if your message is unavoidably complex, email is also a good choice for laying everything out in detail.

Just don't use email if you're looking for an immediate response.

Recently, we hired someone who had never worked remotely before—and she drove me *crazy* with all the emails she sent. I kept asking her to communicate through chat, because I only check email a couple of times a day, but I'm on messaging systems all day long, so … I kept missing information I needed to get sh*t done!

Here's how to handle someone like this—when they email you, copy and paste its content into a chat message and reply that way.

TIP #20: USE YOUR EMAIL REAL ESTATE WISELY

The subject line and first three lines of an email are like the Park Place and Boardwalk killer combo in Monopoly, so don't waste them. You have maybe three seconds to grab your recipient's attention long enough to convey the vital information before they move on to the next message or check their Amazon delivery. So be direct and concise.

> **The subject line and first three lines of an email are like the Park Place and Boardwalk killer combo in Monopoly, so don't waste them.**

If you need a response, an action to be taken, or if the email is just plain urgent, make the subject line an attention grabber. Use asterisks if necessary, and please take the time to delete the forwards (FW: FW: FW:) at the beginning. Similarly, since most email systems preview the first three lines, don't waste this space. Put the key information you need actioned here. Better yet, send a text that you need them to respond to your email.

TIP #21: STOP, STOP WITH THE CC'S

You know those emails where you end up with fifty emails on a thread because all the "To" and "cc" people replied all? Don't be the source of this; try not to clutter other people's inboxes with unnecessary cc's.

Along the same lines, don't add too many people in the "To" line, as they will all think they have to react when maybe they don't. If you have regular emails to a group, take the time to create distribution lists. Nothing shouts online newbie like repeated group emails to identifiable email addresses.

As for those blind copies? Use with caution. If it is really supposed to be a "blind copy," you are better off forwarding the original sent email to the person you secretly want to see the message. Otherwise you risk a "reply all" from the bcc, and your cover will be blown.

Of course, for mass emails with distribution lists, bcc is fine, as long as there are no "To" and "cc" email addresses in the email header.

CHAPTER 4

ALTO IMPACTO: ONLINE MEETINGS & OFFSITES THAT MATTER

Here's the thing about virtual work—it is far more flexible and easier for meetings and events than anything you've experienced before. Now, instead of flying three hundred people into a central location, renting conference rooms and hotel rooms, figuring out evening entertainment and catering, and hauling away flip chart notes that someone has to decipher later … you can do the entire thing online. No airport delays, no jet lag, no contagious people passing on their colds (or worse), no missing your dog-training graduation or other important events … and, when everything is said and done, all content gets recorded for posterity. This is an area where virtual work really shines.

The same thing holds for conventions and larger events. Of course, nothing can replicate the impact of a trade show booth and those suitcases of tchotchkes people haul home, but you can certainly deliver leadership, training, and sales messages to hundreds of people online for a fraction of the cost.

But … here's the thing. Most companies are trying to replicate the in-person experience by moving it online as is. They want to get everyone in front of a screen for eight hours a day over multiple days. One company we talked to didn't even plan on a lunch break because they usually have catering during sessions. This is just brutal, especially for people facilitating these sessions.

You have the opportunity now to rethink and re-engineer the experience. Here are some proven tactics on how to manage meetings and events when nobody is in the same room.

TIP #22: FLEX YOUR VIRTUAL MEETING TIME

From managing hundreds of regional and global online events over the past decade, I can tell you, the maximum anyone should be in an online meeting is four hours (and even that's pushing it—two hours would be better). When they run longer than that, your participants are going to experience significant muscle and eye fatigue, not to mention be tempted by the incredible distractions that come with working remotely. The answer is simple: set shorter-duration meeting blocks on a regular schedule over a longer time period. Even if someone misses a session, you can record everything, and they can catch up later.

Online meetings give you an assortment of advantages, so don't lock yourself into traditional thinking. With virtual events, you can target your message by geography, functional area, or industry. Just avoid Monday mornings and Friday afternoons for these kinds of video marathons!

TIP #23: TEMPLATE EVERYTHING THAT MOVES

When you run a meeting in person, you have much more control—because you literally have a captive audience. In a large conference room, you can ban smartphones, make sure all screens are down, and be far more agile with agendas. When every member of your audience is at a different location, you lose that control.

So, you need to build virtual walls and a structure to keep things on track. This is where templates for meeting agendas, minutes, action items, status updates, quarterly business reviews, and a whole lot more come into play. Make these available from the central dashboard you created, and reinforce on calls where they are and how to find them.

Inevitably, people are going to adapt these templates to their own needs, which is something you should encourage. Meet quarterly, share best practices, agree on new formats, and update your dashboard so you have a continuous improvement process in place.

TIP #24: USE TIME ZONES WISELY

I've worked in New Zealand at 3:00 a.m., in Delhi at midnight, and to be honest, I wasn't sure what time it was in Newfoundland. My point is, when you schedule an online meeting, make sure you take into account everyone's time zone if they vary, so Fred in Oregon doesn't have to get up at 5:00 a.m.—or, worse, Pierre in Paris doesn't have to stay up until 5:00 a.m.!

Try to establish four-hour common slots of time so everyone has a block for meetings and a block for working. This creates uninterrupted time so people can focus without interruption (assuming they have a door).

Consider breaking up large meetings into regional ones as much as possible for everyone's convenience. Rotate meeting times for all-hands-on-deck virtual get-togethers, so everyone has the chance to operate within "normal" business hours. And always, always, *always* remind everyone of an upcoming meeting twenty-four hours in advance.

TIP #25: MAKE IT EASY TO ADD AGENDA ITEMS

Even after an agenda for a meeting has been created, things come up and new items need to be added. So, capture your team's input 24/7 and make it easy to change things up anytime.

Once again, this is where dashboards come in handy. Ours has a link that people can click to submit risks, issues, or ideas, which get automatically added to our meeting agendas. These extra items are then covered during the weekly call, things are reprioritized if need be, and actions assigned. Even though that agenda ends up being very fluid, everything gets captured in that online dashboard, so there's a complete record that can be referred to.

TIP #26: HIT THE RECORD BUTTON

I've been involved in enough meetings where, even if detailed minutes are taken, someone will still want to argue about who really said what during the conversation. There's one simple way to end all those conflicts, and that's by making sure each meeting is recorded. That's a pretty easy thing to accomplish with a virtual team, because most remote meeting tech tools have a record feature. You can even automate that feature in most programs so recording automatically happens.

Laws differ as to whether you need written or oral approval to have a meeting recorded, so double-check on what the legal situation is for you and others who participate. And finally, when you're discussing personnel issues, press the pause button on the recording. Some remarks can come as very expensive Perry Mason moments!

TIP #27: PROTEST POINTLESS MEETINGS

Meetings can be very valuable planning sessions ... or completely unnecessary wastes of time. If it looks like a future confab is likely to be the latter, and if you have been empowered to point out silly work practices, suggest that it be put off or scrapped. Meetings should have a purpose aimed at achieving an outcome, a takeaway, and/or a next step. Otherwise … why do it at all?

"Pointless" includes inviting a whole host of people to a meeting who don't need to be there. Think Marie Kondo when you're putting together the invite list. Get rid of clutter, reduce needless time waste.

> **Meetings should have a purpose aimed at achieving an outcome, a takeaway, and/or a next step. Otherwise … why do it at all?**

And don't take a chunk of valuable work time away from a team member for a call they don't need to be on!

TIP #28: KEEP A SET SCHEDULE

We schedule regular departmental meetings with set agendas. Before each meeting, everyone posts their (hopefully) very succinct status slide in the team meeting space. We block out individual time in our calendars to review the slides before the call. When meeting time comes, if there's little to discuss, everyone gets some time back in their day. If there's a large issue on the agenda, however, we know about it in advance and come to the meeting prepared to go to work.

This kind of regular schedule encourages accountability, reduces interruptions, and also cuts down on ad hoc meetings. That's why there should be a clear expectation built around reporting on assignments and submitting status updates weekly or monthly (or whatever your meeting schedule is). If everyone finds the window is too short between meetings and there's not enough to report, then push out the reporting period. But maybe also look at why there's not enough to report!

TIP #29: DON'T LOSE THE PLOT WITH A WALK

Before the pandemic, "walking meetings" were gaining in popularity. Colleagues would not only talk the talk; they would literally walk the walk as they stretched their legs and discussed concerns.

Some are trying to keep this concept going with virtual meetings, by participating via cell phone while they're out for a stroll. Combining exercise with business isn't a bad idea, but again, just make sure there is some system in place to memorialize what was agreed to, either by recording the call or sending out a simple recap to all concerned after the call. You never want a "he said, she said" moment where someone produces something you didn't agree to, but you can't prove it.

TIP #30: TREAT MEETINGS LIKE CONTRACT DISCUSSIONS

Unlike loosey-goosey meetings in a physical office that allow you to shine in front of the bosses, online loosey-goosey meetings without any real point don't get anyone anywhere. If it's just about on-webcam bonding, that's fine, just realize you are not going to accomplish anything of substance. (I want to put it out here, by the way, that I overdosed on group hugs in the '80s, so now I don't engage in them either virtually or in person!)

But let's assume you are trying to accomplish something of substance in a meeting. First of all, set a strong agenda. If appropriate, have mechanisms for the team to add items to it. Even with that agenda in place, things can still go sideways. Somebody might decide they want to pontificate on their favorite sports team for ten minutes. If that happens, gently steer them back to the agenda (or if you want to be evil, just mute them and claim you did it by accident).

And make sure you get opinions from everyone. Since you'll often have a mix of extroverts, introverts, and different management levels in the meeting, sometimes not every person feels comfortable sharing. Ironically, the people who don't share are usually the ones you need to hear from. So, consider implementing anonymous voting and comment-and-question input forms. You would be amazed how engagement increases, especially from people who would not otherwise speak up.

Finally, just like a contract, you need to document what the team decided, who agreed to do what by when, and what things need to be looked after. And all this needs to be reiterated and agreed upon, put in meeting minutes, and those meeting minutes distributed and followed up on.

TIP #31: DON'T DRIVE YOURSELF TO DISTRACTION

Back in 2012, Siemens[3] found that 75 percent of people on virtual calls were doing *anything* other than listening to the call. Imagine what that statistic is like today. Even when everyone's on camera, people could be doing things like looking at their phones (which they hold just out of video range) or proofing the first draft of their screenplay (which they're pretending is paperwork for the meeting).

---

3   "Siemens Enterprise Communications Survey Highlights Untapped Potential of Teams," PR Newswire, October 24, 2012, https://www.prnewswire.com/news-releases/siemens-enterprise-communications-survey-highlights-untapped-potential-of-teams-175576081.html.

Train yourself to cut down distractions (this is where that office door comes in handy!) to improve productivity. Turn off your phone and notifications and encourage others in the meeting to do the same thing. Otherwise, someone is going to ask you something and there will be that dead air as everyone waits for you to respond and you blame your mute button but everyone knows you were doing something else.

If you find yourself not paying attention, ask yourself, do you really need to be on the call?

> **If you find yourself not paying attention, ask yourself, do you really need to be on the call?**

TIP #32: END WHEN YOU'RE DONE ...

With virtual, you have the opportunity to do more with less. Meetings don't have to run the full time allotted. We see many cases where the agenda items have been covered and someone pipes up with a new topic that most of the meeting participants have no interest in—and the call drags across the finish line.

This is the Marie Kondo approach again. By removing clutter, increasing organization and meeting preparation, and sticking to exactly what you need to get done, you are going to give a lot of people back time in their working day. Which will make you an online rock star.

So, try a fifteen-minute meeting instead of thirty minutes and a forty-five-minute meeting instead of an hour. Nothing ventured, nothing gained.

CHAPTER 5

THE X-TEAM: RUNNING BUSINESS PROJECTS

arvard Business Review did a study that found that a whopping 75 percent of cross-functional teams ("X-Teams") are dysfunctional![4] No wonder! Cross-functional teams are usually composed of people reporting to different managers, usually in different locations, who do not report to the team lead. You might not even run the team—your manager may have just placed you on it because their manager placed them on it. Sometimes it feels like losing a game of hot potato when you end

---

4   Behnam Tabrizi, "75% of Cross-Functional Teams Are Dysfunctional," *Harvard Business Review*, June 23, 2015, https://hbr.org/2015/06/75-of-cross-functional-teams-are-dysfunctional.

up in this position.

This chapter is for more advanced workers. It assumes you know the fundamentals of how to scope a project, build a charter, create a plan to keep a project on track, and use project tools to do this.

What's tricky about cross-functional projects, even in the best of times, is they add work to an already-packed day job, so cross-functional meetings tend to have highly distracted team members. For this reason, and the distributed nature of the team, they are never easy to manage. Even so, there are things you can do to tame the beast and keep team members engaged.

Here are some tips to help your X-Team excel.

TIP #33: PLAN WITH WHITEBOARDS

When everyone's working remotely, project planning can be tricky. You can't all just pile into the conference room and brainstorm your way through lunch. That's why you should consider implementing online whiteboarding tools like Miro or InVision to help visually communicate ideas, draw and link process flows (allowing others to add their own online sticky notes), move things around and brainstorm. You'll find, even though you're not all in the same room, your team can easily innovate, create, and organize through these kinds of free-form platforms.

TIP #34: GET STAKEHOLDERS ON BOARD EARLY

You need to make an effort to engage all stakeholders early, even if they won't be involved until much later in the process. This way, you don't risk someone popping up at the last minute and stopping your progress in its tracks. Better to know this is going to happen at the beginning stages of a project, so you can plan work-arounds or cancel the project entirely.

Who are stakeholders? At a minimum, they are each manager that your team reports to. If your team senses that their boss is invested in the project, they will work extra hard to generate great ideas and make it a priority to meet all objectives. Stakeholders can also include end users, salespeople, influencers, execs, and/or others with the power of approval. They might not even be part of your company and could be an external regulatory agency or customer.

Stakeholder Status Report Example

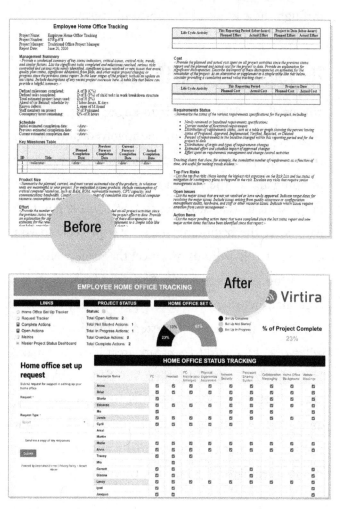

Figure 3. Status report before and after

For all these groups, engage early. You need to do more than generate a RACI chart, you need to create a comprehensive stakeholder communications plan. As shown in figure 3, everything that goes out, including reports, presentations, and status, must be crafted to be easily understood and quickly digested—so a stakeholder doesn't have to dig for the information. You want them to raise their hand early and let you know there's an issue.

TIP #35: UNDERSTAND WHO REALLY MAKES DECISIONS

Never assume you know who actually has the final say on an outcome. We had a project once where every Monday, the VP would set a direction and every Friday, after a mysterious steering committee meeting, he would abruptly change that direction, like a weather vane spinning in the wind. Eventually we had to shut the project down until we were able to interact with the real decision makers.

> **Never assume you know who actually has the final say on an outcome.**

Situations like that mean you should establish right away how decisions are going to be made and who must be involved. Do your team members have the authority to make decisions? Are you going to need to engage their managers or other stakeholders? Whether it's someone high up the food chain making the call or whether decisions are made by consensus, make sure to engage early and communicate often to head off potential blockages.

TIP #36: MAKE IT EASY FOR NEWBIES TO GET ON BOARD

I read one consultant who said that in order to be effective, a cross-functional team needs to work together for at least two years. This, frankly, is poppycock. Cross-functional team members change all the time. Between medical leaves, corporate reorganizations, job changes, and strategy pivots, you can end up with a constant churn of new team members. That's why it's essential that someone new to the project has the ability to get quickly up to speed and be a productive team member. And here's where dashboards come in handy again.

A project dashboard, with a summary of the project charter and objectives, along with a project overview, schedule, risk, collaboration links, metrics, team members, meeting recordings, and other relevant information, is a great way to bring new people up to speed quickly. It also provides an instant snapshot that also empowers stakeholders and executives to monitor anything you're working on. Create one for your team and you'll be treated like you deserve to be—a project rock star!

TIP #37: THROW OUT WHAT YOU LEARNED ABOUT MEETING MINUTES

Traditional meeting minutes based on Robert's Rules of Order spend an inordinate amount of time laying out who was at the meeting, when it was held, who called the meeting to order, etc. etc. etc.

You don't have the luxury of this format for online communications. You need the reader to immediately understand project decisions, risks, who is accountable for what, what their deadlines are, and when the next meeting is. *After* that, you can list all the detailed information. For an example, look at the meeting minute template in figure 4, which you can download from virtira.com/resources.

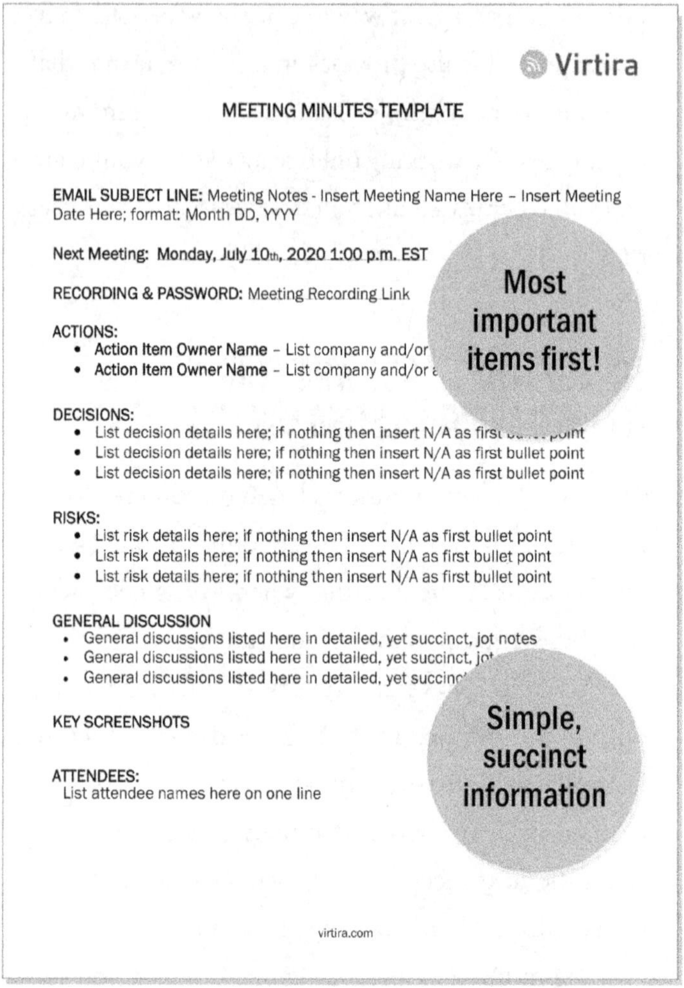
Virtira

MEETING MINUTES TEMPLATE

EMAIL SUBJECT LINE: Meeting Notes - Insert Meeting Name Here – Insert Meeting Date Here; format: Month DD, YYYY

Next Meeting: Monday, July 10th, 2020 1:00 p.m. EST

RECORDING & PASSWORD: Meeting Recording Link

ACTIONS:
- **Action Item Owner Name** – List company and/or
- **Action Item Owner Name** – List company and/or

DECISIONS:
- List decision details here; if nothing then insert N/A as first bullet point
- List decision details here; if nothing then insert N/A as first bullet point
- List decision details here; if nothing then insert N/A as first bullet point

RISKS:
- List risk details here; if nothing then insert N/A as first bullet point
- List risk details here; if nothing then insert N/A as first bullet point
- List risk details here; if nothing then insert N/A as first bullet point

GENERAL DISCUSSION
- General discussions listed here in detailed, yet succinct, jot notes
- General discussions listed here in detailed, yet succinct, jo
- General discussions listed here in detailed, yet succin

KEY SCREENSHOTS

ATTENDEES:
List attendee names here on one line

virtira.com

Figure 4. Meeting minutes template example

TIP #38: WORK IT TO GET ATTENTION ON YOUR PROJECT

If I were to emphasize one tip over all the others in this book, it would be this one. Especially with X-Teams, in shifting organizations, you need to focus on selling ideas and telling stories, so that people engage with your communications.

> You need to assume no one pays attention during meetings, reads any of the follow-up messaging, and sees status updates or risks.

You need to assume no one pays attention during meetings, reads any of the follow-up messaging, and sees status updates or risks. If you follow up and create communications based on this perspective, you'll focus on conveying the most information with the fewest words and ideally using images. You need impactful, succinct headlines to convey what the recipient needs to understand. If they are interested in digging further, they can do this. Remember, for most people this initiative is in addition to an already overloaded day job, so communicate accordingly.

TIP #39: ACCENTUATE ACCOUNTABILITY

Don't ever think accountability is going to automatically happen or be handled by the Remote Work Fairy (her name is Esmeralda, by the way, and she's just not dependable). Instead, send action item reminders before the meeting and follow up afterward with new assignments, so everyone is clear on their responsibilities. Designate someone to take minutes during the meeting on items related to the agenda and have that person send them out in a timely fashion (in other words, not in the middle of the *next* meeting).

TIP #40: ASSUME NO ONE WILL DELIVER ANYTHING ON TIME

Following on the previous tip, you need to be proactive in reminding people of what you need from them, because otherwise they'll forget or it'll be shoved way down to the bottom of their to-do list.

I have a couple of people working for me, who will remind me one year, two months, two weeks, a week, and the day before an action item is due. They make sure whatever it is stays top of mind. I'm sure if they had to send someone to my door with surprise balloons to remind me of my action items or hire a plane with a banner to fly past my house, they would do so. Encourage everyone to follow up like this, and you'll see things move much faster.

Dashboards can be a big help in facilitating follow-up because you can add auto-reminders for tasks that must be acknowledged with a click. If that click doesn't happen, then you can follow up (by message, text, phone call, LinkedIn message, showing up at the dog park, whatever) to make sure things are moving forward.

TIP #41: EMPOWER EMPLOYEES TO ESCALATE ISSUES AND RISK

If you're a Monty Python fan, then you undoubtedly know one of their most famous sketches, in which John Cleese plays the Minister of Silly Walks. With his endless legs, he pulls off the most ridiculous stride you've ever seen ... but as he silly-walks down the street, passers-by act like what he's doing is the most normal thing in the world.

Watching silly walks and saying nothing is exactly what it feels like being an unempowered team member tasked with making a VP pet project succeed. Over the years, my team has estimated that at least 50 percent of the business projects fail because leadership demands unrealistic, unattainable goals. Show me a spectacular project failure, and I'll show you a leader who set a completely unrealistic date, along with a big consulting company who knew this from day one and still took the $200 million to build a disaster.

Usually, the people who actually have to try to pull off Mission: Impossible know it's ... well, impossible. But few ever speak up because, well, it's the executives pushing these impossible projects, and trust me, no one is going to risk their job by calling a COO on the carpet.

In virtual teams, especially cross-functional ones, this reticence to point out the silly walk increases. The quiet hallway conversations with influencers, where you can hint at impending disaster, don't happen, and it just isn't the same via messaging or the phone.

So, I'm going to suggest this, although I have never seen an organization implement it—empower your employees to speak up about these not-yet but soon-to-be disasters. Especially now, no one can afford failure. Suggest to leadership that an anonymous early warning system be created to flag potential risk. Involve a leader who doesn't have a vested outcome in the project with the power to come in and remediate the situation.

TIP #42: DON'T CAUSE EXECUTIVES TO LOSE FACE

If egos prevent that risk mitigation system I just described from being taken seriously, and your team is wedged between a rock and a hard place in terms of taking on an undoable project, you need to somehow create a success.

If you can, break the beast into smaller milestones that can be recognized and enjoyed as a victory. Rather than a global rollout, run a regional pilot where you know it'll be successful. That way, if the thing is canceled or goes sideways, you'll still have a series of successful results, and you'll make your department and your VP look great.

CHAPTER 6

IN IT FOR THE LONG HAUL: WHEN REMOTE WORKING BECOMES THE "NEW NORMAL"

This pandemic may result in something I've advocated for years—more people working remotely. In most cases, there is no reason for workers to travel to the office to do tasks they can accomplish just as easily in a home office. Why not give workers a break from endless commutes? Why not offer them a preferable form of work-life balance that in the past only existed for a lucky few? The outcomes are overwhelmingly positive: virtual workers are frequently less stressed, happier, and more productive.

As for the companies? Not to mention saving tons of carbon a year, businesses end up saving on infrastructure, office space, and have a pool of talent available from a much broader geographic area. Executives are discovering these unexpected benefits for themselves—and some are making permanent tele-commuting adjustments.

The most challenging part of working remotely for most people is the lack of meeting someone in person. You no longer have accidental run-ins with others in office hallways that often yield important discussions. Now the only thing you run into is that file cabinet you keep meaning to move.

If working full-time from home ends up being your new norm, here are a few final tips to make your virtual job as productive as possible.

TIP #43: CREATE AN ERGONOMICALLY HEALTHY SETUP

The last thing you need after surviving COVID-19 is ending up with neck or back pain or carpal tunnel syndrome. You can find thousands of articles and videos to help guide you in creating a desk setup that won't bring on the pain down the line. You should invest in a separate monitor and keyboard and not work from your laptop if this is going to be a long-term solution. Our company hires ergonomic experts to do a presentation for all-hands-on-deck calls; then we adapt the recording for our new employee training. If people still are having problems with their setup, we'll ask a specialist to do a video check to make sure it's as physically comfortable as possible.

TIP #44: SUPERSIZE YOUR TEAM'S SOCIAL NETWORKING

Remember our ten cats in the field? Well, maybe they'd work together better if they agreed to meet up in a specific spot every so often to beef up their bonding. Yes, I know, you can't expect tabbies to keep tabs on each other, but you should be able to get to know your teammates a little better.

You can do that by establishing and nurturing internal social networks so people can have random, non-work-related dialogues about important things like the next *Game of Thrones* spinoff or tips to keep the kids occupied during your work hours. There should also be a dedicated announcement channel (this shouldn't be interactive—no comments allowed and content should be controlled), as well as an "I need help" channel so anyone can reach out to the team for assistance on tech, project parameters, etc.

Your team should also make an effort to get to know each other on a more personal level and find common shared interests and experiences. That helps develop trust and allows for more candid and open dialogues.

If you have new people on the team, make sure to do regular introductions and include hobbies and personal interests to make the person more real. We have a standard introduction template for new hires to help build structure around this process.

A great way to create a sense of belonging and build efficacy in a team is to highlight individual achievements.

A great way to create a sense of belonging and build efficacy in a team is to highlight individual achievements. We have an online form for people to recognize others going the extra mile and a monthly newsletter with a "Kudos" section.

TIP #45: CONTINUOUSLY CONFIRM YOUR CULTURE

As a completely virtual company, we've had to adapt bricks-and-mortar management methods to remote work over the past decade. Our own internal culture is defined by four simple pillars—passion, mission, guiding principles, and core values. These, as well as our commitment to diversity, respect, and ethics, are communicated as part of our new-hire training to anyone joining our company. We also feature these on rotating slides as people are joining monthly all-hands meetings.

You should consider doing the same with your team moving forward. Creating common purpose and values strengthens bonding and helps put everyone on the same page. Just know that this step must come *after* you successfully transition to work online. You can't build culture in chaos. Once your team is virtually competent and organized, let the culture building begin!

TIP #46: PUT SOME PERSONALITY INTO THE MIX

In order to get to know each other better, a fun exercise is for everyone to take personality tests and share each other's results. Better yet, have an online team session and have everyone use color-coded stickies to guess each other's results. There are a lot of fantastic free ones online (such as the DiSC Assessment, 16Personalities, or the Myers-Briggs Type Indicator), and they're a lot more accurate than tarot cards and astrology (in my opinion anyway). Understanding each other's communication styles gives all of you "hidden keys" on how best to deal with each other—because you learn what your team members do and don't respond to.

TIP #47: JUST SAY NO TO FIRE DRILLS

I'm not talking about a literal fire drill, so don't worry about having to stand in your driveway for five minutes until an alarm dies down. No, in this context, fire drills are urgent requests and unplanned last-minute deadlines. For some reason, these skyrocket with remote work.

Here's the dirty little secret about fire drills—they are usually completely bogus. If I had a dollar for the number of times I had someone ask me on a Friday afternoon for something first thing Monday morning … that they didn't even look at until Thursday … well, I would own Tahiti and maybe a few other islands too.

Last-minute "I need it yesterday" assignments are the result of poor planning and can cause burnout (burnout—ironic for a "fire drill," right?). They take you away from your real work, slam your calendar, and usually end up with you spending a whole weekend in front of your screen. Ask yourself before you accept another one of these dictums, "Is it really worth putting my work and personal life on hold to deal with one specific and time-consuming demand (that the person probably does not need as urgently as they think they do)?"

Learn to say no. If you're like me and want to make things happen, this goes against your grain. It's not the easiest thing to do. But we need to train ourselves, then train our managers in order to be a catalyst for change within the organization. So, when Mr. Manager texts you on a Friday afternoon to ask you to work all weekend and you've got plans, let them know you're headed out of town … but would be glad to tackle it Monday morning. Usually, surprisingly, this is fine.

If this gets you in a sweat, remember how long it took them to review your work the last five times this happened. Remember also, if you've been accepting these unreasonable requests for a while, it's going to take some time to change your behavior and even more time to change your manager's behavior. So, take baby steps and ease into it.

TIP #48: CHECK IN WITH YOUR TEAM REGULARLY

There are many good reasons to check in with everyone on a regular basis—but the biggest motivator should be when someone goes "dark" and stops responding. They could be struggling—or worse, they may be upset or feel hurt by some virtual interaction that might have been completely misunderstood. This is a situation where you can't afford the drama to escalate. If you don't feel comfortable calling the person directly to see what's going on, try asking HR or a third party to resolve the matter—before things go really sideways.

TIP #49: STAY BALANCED

At the same time, don't forget to have a life and one that won't kill you. When you work at home, all sorts of lines can end up getting crossed. You could find yourself up at 2:00 a.m. finishing up a report. And you could end up ignoring important parts of your personal life, simply because your office is now in your home. Look for ways to integrate work into your life, instead of allowing it to do a hostile takeover. If you want to maintain regular work hours because that's how you're the most efficient, that's fine. For me, work is just part of my life—not the biggest part, but it's how I pay for the rest of it. This may seem like an extreme example, but on my way up Everest, I knew there was Wi-Fi at Tengboche Monastery bakery at 12,600 feet. So I hunkered down an extra day, cleared out my inbox, and kept trekking.

> **Look for ways to integrate work into your life, instead of allowing it to do a hostile takeover.**

TIP #50: CONTINUE BUILDING BEST PRACTICES

Build best practice and failure sharing into your cultural DNA. Be an organization that recognizes silly walks and not-so-silly walks and incorporates lessons learned from failures through planned retrospective sessions.[5]

One of our guiding principles is to "Question Everything." So even if something seems like it is ingrained and everyone has been doing it a particular way for decades, haul it out and put it to task if there's a better way to do it.

When something works, everyone should know why and how it worked, hopefully to the extent where they can replicate the mighty deed themselves. Even more important is to celebrate failure, even if you have to use anonymous feedback forms to find out what those failures are. If people are thinking outside the box and trying new things, of course things are going to fail. But there might be a gold nugget in that failure that could shape a future success.

---

5   Check out http://www.funretrospectives.com/ for ideas.

CONCLUSION

When you work in an office setting, you're in a location dedicated entirely to work. You never forget you're on the job because you're *at* the job.

But working from home creates a different psychological vibe. Suddenly, you're navigating around your spouse, kids, pets, and whatever else is going on in your household. In short, your surroundings are more about your personal life, rather than your professional one.

If you can get over that mental hurdle and discipline yourself enough to do your job, you can find this is a wonderful opportunity to integrate all aspects of your life as never before. Want to go to your kid's soccer game? Then take the afternoon off and knock out that report at night. Want to travel across North America in a van for two months? Go ahead and catch up on work on the road.

Cynthia returning to the office.

There's no question the pandemic is a horrible event in our history, but nevertheless, some positive things will come out of its aftermath. One of them will be an increase in telecommuting—and that will make many people's lives a lot easier. I hope you are among that lucky group and find great success in your new role. And more than anything, I hope you GET SH*T DONE!

If you're interested in more information about best practices in working and managing remotely, I invite you to visit our company's website at virtira.com.

ACKNOWLEDGMENTS

I would like to thank the incredibly bright, talented individuals on the Virtira and Sales Beacon teams, from whom I'm constantly learning new best practices. Their passion to get the most done in the least time, mixed with common sense and real-world experience, has resulted in some of the most practical, easy-to-implement ways to improve virtual team performance available today.

I would also like to thank my Grade 11 English teacher, Mr. Lawson, who introduced me to *The Elements of Style* and the wonder of saying more with fewer words. Similarly, Nancy Duarte's numerous books and videos on transforming presentations into engaging stories have been a foundation for our virtual communications for over twenty years.

We can't forget the support of the Nova Scotia Business Inc. and the Government of Canada export programs for supporting us with mentorship and marketing funding to grow our international market exposure. Our clients, who are trailblazers like us, have been willing to adopt our methods, because they continue to see the revenue and productivity payoffs. Finally, to Susan Cain and her Ted Talk and book *Quiet: The Power of Introverts in a World That Can't Stop Talking*. I wish I'd read her book when I was ten. It was transformational.

ABOUT THE AUTHOR

Cynthia Spraggs was never cut out to work in an office. She grew up in a small town on Vancouver Island in Canada, and while her business school classmates were finding jobs in downtown cubicles, she happily worked her way through university in the BC Parks Branch and on fishing boats. Because she was extremely introverted, and preferred thinking to speaking, Cynthia went into IT sales in the '80s to develop her speaking skills (and spend as much time out of the office as possible).

After stints with large consulting and tech companies during which she completed her MBA and research into telecommuting, she consulted to clients across the globe, running RFP and business startup projects—all while trekking across Asia and

South America. With no need to meet in person, her location opportunities were endless.

Later, while working virtually for a Fortune 500 IT company, she developed a sales project management office and managed a large team facilitating and optimizing global cross-functional projects.

She took over Virtira (then Sales Beacon) in 2011 and meshed her academic research, team best practices, and her own remote work experience into a completely virtual company. These best practices for optimizing remote team performance continue to be innovated. Living a somewhat nomadic and "bi-coastal" lifestyle, she, her husband, and their two small dogs commute between the west and east coasts of Canada. Her most enduring passion has been providing opportunities for rural residents to have meaningful careers without leaving home, as well as helping clients achieve less stress via the ever-elusive work-life balance. And if you ask anyone who knows her, she has no plan on stopping anytime soon.